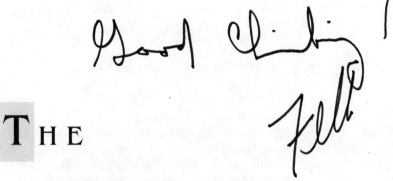

THE MOUNTAINS OF OUR LIVES

Every Man May Take a Different Path
to Reach the Summit But Many Will
Encounter the Same Roadblocks

GRANVILLE KNIGHT, JR.

The Mountains of Our Lives

Copyright © 2006 by Granville Knight, Jr.

First Edition

10 9 8 7 6 5 4 3 2 1

To order:
gcknight5bar@aol.com or www.knightmountains.com

Library of Congress Catalog Card Number: 2006929166

PAW PRINT PRESS
Carol J. Rhodes, Editor/Publisher
8720 Memorial Drive
Houston, TX 77024-7011
www.paw-print-press.com

ISBN 0-9779278-0-6

Printed in the United States of America
by Morgan Printing in Austin, Texas

To

My Wife,
Elaine

My Children
Wade, Amy, & Brady

✠

And

the thousands of people who are tired

of climbing mountains: those who

recognize they

still have so much to give,

but who just

need a little help in finding a different road

than the one on which they are

currently traveling.

CONTENTS

Appreciation

My deepest gratitude goes to these friends for their kindness, insight, encouragement, and inspiration:

The Reverend Stanley Telchin, whose presentation in 1981, *The Mountains of Your Life*, planted the seed for my research.

George S. Glass, MD, a psychiatrist, who gave me invaluable advice and some gentle pushes to put my thoughts down on paper.

Debbie Longano, PhD, a psychologist, who for ten years has counseled me, advised me, and always given me a path to follow.

The tragedy of life is not that it ends too soon,

but that we wait so long to begin it.

— W. M. Lewis

INTRODUCTION

As we approach the time in our lives defined as middle age, there is a possibility that the excitement of job, family life, or a night out with the boys does not have quite the same meaning as in earlier years. We begin to wonder: *Where am I? Am I going down hill? Is this a permanent feeling? What lies ahead?*

These feelings are normal, natural, and predictable. Since most of us have never had anyone, teacher, parent, or minister, explain the anxieties we may have to face, we are simply at sea without a rudder.

The irony of this is that the second half of our life should be as exciting as the first half. We all face potential problems if we are unwilling to recognize that changes do occur.

We need to slow down and ask ourselves: *Where am I now? Where am I going?*

Bob Buford's book, *Half Time,* quotes Peter Drucker as saying, "People in their mid-forties find their work can no longer be challenging. They need a new stimulus."

Patrick M. Morley's classic book, *The Seven Seasons of a Man's Life,* says, "Burnout is one of the most common reasons men are stressed out and feel fatigued all the time. Some medical professionals estimate up to ninety percent of all visits to the doctor are the result of burnout and stress."

Jim Conway's book, *Men in Mid-Life Crisis*, explains "The man approaching midlife has some strange and difficult times ahead of him." You may negotiate the earlier walk in unfamiliar territory with little trouble, but by midlife you are more apt to feel like Humpty Dumpty. It is a time of high risk for divorce, affairs, depression, alcohol, anger, frustration, and rebellion."

In *Life is Not a Game of Perfect* by Dr. Bob Rotella and Bob Cullen, they simply say, "Find your real talent and make it work for you." Easier said than done!

Gail Sheehy's best seller, *Understanding Men's Passages: Discovering the New Map of Men's Lives,* sums up the problem this way: "Men think when they achieve certain things, then they will be happy. But it is not all the titles and accomplishments that matter and when those external achievements fail to provide meaning and joyfulness, men become frustrated, confused, angry, and ashamed to admit it." She further says, "These unsettling periods of change will likely let a man slide into depression. It is a downward movement, inch by inch."

I admit to having had most of these feelings and problems. At age fifty, after twenty-five years of sales and management, I began to realize my normal, enthusiastic approach to the world of business was waning. I asked myself, "*Is this simply a temporary setback? If I keep on pushing, will my enthusiasm return?*" If I had known then what I have learned from twenty years of study, research, and interviews, I could have saved myself many years of self-doubt.

Men simply do not ask for directions, in traffic or on life's road. I instinctively assumed I was the only one on the planet who was experiencing life changes. One phone call to a medical doctor or psychologist who specializes in men's mid-life problems would not only have eased my state of mind, but saved my family years of having to guess what mood I might be in next. Too bad Debbie Longano, PhD, was not in my life sooner. I know of no other viewpoint which is as destructive and leads to so many problems as, "This is my problem and I'm damn well strong enough to handle it myself."

But men usually question why they should ask for help when they can handle these *temporary* feelings on their own. I needed to understand that I could not change the normal feelings I was having as I moved from one stage of my life to another. There were some mountains out there I had never seen before or certainly never had to climb alone. And now I realize that lurking in my future are even more mountains to encounter and ascend as my life moves forward. Does this mean that ahead is intense therapy or medications to help me cope? No way!

The following chapters have been written with the help of numerous individuals and many books, but are primarily a result of listening to people who have genuinely and honestly talked about their situation in life, and who have been unable to come up with the answers which would resolve their worries. All of my research is from a personal prospective. I have not taken classes in psychology or had any formal training in human behavior.

My sincere desire is that if you come away with at least one thought from this book which will help you climb the next mountain—and there will be one—with more understanding and ease, my efforts will all have been worthwhile. Good climbing!

⸶

Have you ever started a path? No one seems willing to do this. We don't mind using existing paths, but we rarely start new ones.
Do it today.

—George Carlin

CHAPTER ONE

IT'S JUST THE WAY
MEN ARE

When I was forty, my doctor advised me that a man in his forties shouldn't play tennis. I heeded his advice carefully, and could hardly wait until I reached fifty to start again.

— Hugh L. Black

I T'S JUST THE WAY

MEN ARE

At age twenty-one, did any of us ever give a minute's thought to getting old or that one day our chosen career might cease to be challenging or important? Likewise, we probably never expected to have such problems as decreased libido, the inability to run three miles every day, choosing a nap instead of sex, hair loss, or a doctor saying, "Sir, let's talk about your high blood pressure."

But now that some or all of these things are occurring, have we shared these concerns with *anyone*? The answer, sad to say, is a universal *No.* Because, *it's just the way men are.*

Specifically, for the first half of our lives, men are given a feather in their cap for putting on a mask of compliance and walking the same beaten path day after day. At this point, things may appear rather easy and uncomplicated, with little need for directions.

Too, most men have visions and goals which keep them moving at a fast pace. We tend to think there is some magic destination down the road where we will *finally* arrive and find total peace and happiness: when I get a new Mercedes—when I get my next promotion—when my kids are out of college—when I reach retirement . . . It is so easy to get stuck as we reach midlife, however. Stuck in the same job, same friends, same parties . . . we not only know everyone there, but know pretty well what the conversations are going to be about.

In *Understanding Men's Passages: Discovering the New Map of Men's Lives,* Gail Sheehy says, "As you reach midlife, life is like a golf game. As you get older, add about ten strokes to your game because there are some traps out there you never thought of before."

What she is saying is that even though our lives go right along, there will be mental and physical changes never before defined for us. These are the mountains of our lives. Jobs come, go, or get downsized. Children come, go, and often come back. A health problem comes, goes, and then five more come to take its place! Wives go back to work, or quit work, or the marriage in general is just not working out . . . the things which gave us so much excitement in the past twenty-five years no longer do.

When was the last time you heard a man say, "Life is a series of changes and we need to realize each new phase is going to be more exciting and rewarding than the last?" Most men do not connect the dots between change and growth. Rather than seeing it as a positive in respect to inner development, we commonly associate change with sacrifices, compromises, being left behind, or failing. And, we certainly would never think of confiding those negative, bothersome thoughts to someone else. No, *it's just the way men are.*

Tom Brokaw, who at age sixty-one had anchored the NBC Nightly News for eighteen years, had a notion of retirement, but kept his plans to himself. "I don't have a timetable," said Brokaw. "I'm not preparing to retire. I don't want to jump the gun here or anything. But you know, when you get to be my age and my station in life, obviously you think, well, gosh, what do I want to do next, and at what pace? So, that's kind of where I am. I'm just turning these things over. Life is about phases and stages, different seasons. It may be time for me to move on and do some other things I want to do."

The famous golfer, Curtis Strange, during an interview in 2002, was quoted, "You never lose the will to win. But sometimes you lose the will to do all the things you have to do to prepare to win. And then you have to move on."

This is why it is so important for us to slow down and ask ourselves, "Where am I now, and where am I going?" We are not supposed to have voids in our life. God did not make us that way. He gave us time and talents and showed us ways to use them in order to move ahead, but it is up to us to adjust the game plan to keep us vital.

There is a widely shared cultural assumption that life levels off when we are in our fifties or sixties, and then it begins to go downhill. If we act on this premise, we may already see ourselves in a rocking chair on the front porch. Society would have us believe there is a time at which we have enough "points" so that we will feel we have *arrived*. So we continue to run and sweat and climb to reach our own self-perceived goals. When we finally do reach the top, chances are we may experience an empty feeling. Were we climbing the wrong mountain? Life is not a mountain which has a summit, nor is it a game with a final score. Rather, life is a whole mountain range of ups and downs, challenges, and changes.

Roy L. Smith, author of more than sixty books about life, the Bible, and religion, makes it very clear:

As a man grows older—

- he values the voice of experience more and the voice of prophecy less.
- he finds more of life's wealth in the common pleasures—home, health, children.
- he thinks more about the worth of men and less about their wealth.
- he begins to appreciate his own father a little more.

- he boasts less and boosts more.
- he hurries less and usually makes more progress.
- he puts the friendship of God in higher esteem.

It is important to understand that life still has more to offer us and we have more to offer to life. If we look at our lives the same way as we do the beginning of a new day or the passing of one season of the year to another, we will quickly recognize change is necessary, natural, and inevitable.

We frequently forget there is no *final destination* which will give us complete satisfaction. The *true joy* is in the trip. We must relish the moment, and live life to the fullest as we move along. As it says in Psalm 118:24, *"This is the day which the Lord hath made; we shall rejoice and be glad in it."*

The problems of today are not what frustrate men. Instead, they are the *regrets over yesterday* and the *fear of tomorrow*. Research has shown that men over the age of forty have a much harder time making the ascent from the first half of their lives into the second half than do women. Women mostly feel regret over losing their youthful appearance, while men mostly feel dread—dread of being bored, dread of possibly being alone in later years, dread of losing their mental capacities—it is like being on stage and suddenly losing your voice.

In the first half of our lives when *success* is our foremost concern, we are unlikely to pay much attention to some of the things which would clear the way for the second half.

The following are some subtle indicators of change which may have already occurred:

1. Deciding it is not necessary to be the company's sales leader again this year.
2. Dinner with family is more important than entertaining clients.
3. Not wanting to spend more time away from home when given the chance for a promotion.
4. Taking time to read a good book is really not so bad.
5. Making money is still important, but being with a grandchild is more fun.
6. Asking, how much more do I need?
7. Recognizing the need for a new challenge.
8. Going to church becomes more important than playing golf.
9. Taking a year off suddenly seems like a good idea.
10. Writing a book or taking an art course becomes appealing.

Be aware that changes in attitude and perception such as these may happen anytime, anywhere, and often when least expected.

As we move from one mountain peak to another, there are going to be valleys and ravines in between. The question is: how are we going to handle these complex events?

We have two options:

· Let changes control us and live the rest of our lives in a confused state, or

· Accept change, talk about our feelings and frustrations, and have a more exciting life than ever before.

We Are the Only Ones Who Can Make This Choice!

☩

Happiness is a direction, not a place.

—Sydney J. Harris

CHAPTER TWO

MOVING FROM SUCCESS TO SIGNIFICANCE

A man doesn't grow old because he has lived a certain *number of years; he grows old the minute he deserts his ideals.*

— General Douglas McArthur

Moving from
Success to
Significance

SUCCESS lies in *what we do*.
SIGNIFICANCE lies in *who we are*.

Very few people realize how hard it is to make the transition from a life of striving to succeed to a life of striving to be meaningful. *Success* lies in achieving our goals based on varying degrees of social interactions with family, friends, and our profession. This natural behavior serves well to give us an early sense of direction, but gives little or no insight into what we truly stand for and our true reason for existence. *Significance*, on the other hand, lies in what we believe in, what we stand for, and what we would die for.

Unfortunately, we have grown up in a world that keeps score. This is okay as long as we remember our score will soon be forgotten and that the bar continues to rise. From the time we were very young, we have been conditioned to the idea that the way to win friends, recognitions, and rewards is to accomplish great things. Too many times others measure us by the income level we have attained—what we do for a living, the church we attend, the clubs we belong to, where we live, the kind of car we drive, the schools our children go to—all of which, at the time, are normal and necessary incentives to keep us interested and interesting.

Significance often takes a back seat because there are usually no immediate awards. Somehow, working at a food bank, teaching Sunday School, or visiting someone in the hospital, does not carry the same glamour as having your name appear in the society page of the local newspaper.

Learning to play golf is a very good example of how our society has become result-oriented. Each amateur is given a handicap, and is immediately judged by his handicap which is prominently posted on the bulletin board of the golf club. While this is not bad, it only lets us know about the golfer's athletic ability, but leaves us clueless about what he considers important, or whether or not he would be a compatible or congenial golfing partner.

The accumulation of wealth, power, influence, and prestige are self-gratifying, but may not satisfy a man's need to be significant in a lasting way. In *The Man in the Mirror*, Patrick M. Morley explains, "The difference between self-gratification and significance is found in the motive and attitude, not in the task." His significance test is simple: "Does what I am about to do contribute to the welfare of others in a demonstration of faith, love, obedience and service to Christ?"

As we grow older, there is generally a deep-seated desire to move from success to significance, but it is not that easy to make the necessary changes. These are the mountains of our lives, and most men do not know what route to take to get over them. When the fast track we have been on all our adult life is not as stimulating as it once was, we may also find we no longer have the energy or desire to do the required tasks which would keep us at the top. Deep inside, we begin to slowly recognize the need for a new path.

Bob Buford, in his book *Half-Time*, lists eleven important indications that some life changes may be in order:

1. The thrill of closing a major deal is not what it was ten years ago.

2. A younger associate is nipping at your heels and you choose to help him rather than try to stay ahead of him.

3. You spend a lot of time thinking what it might be like to start over or move down to a less responsible

15

position which would give you more control of your life.

4. You have a secure position, yet you are scanning the want ads and openings listed in professional journals.

5. You speculate more about what makes the client tick than how to sell him on a proposal.

6. You envy the guy who walked away from his job to spend more time with his family and in the ministry work he has been dreaming about.

7. You use up all your vacation days and start taking some comp time as well.

8. You begin to ask yourself, "How much is enough?"

9. The boss' hint of a promotion doesn't motivate you as much as it used to.

10. You've been thinking very seriously about starting your own business.

11. One day your son says, "Get a life, Dad."

The question, then, for us to consider is two-fold.

- Are we convinced we want to be more significant than successful?

- What changes do we have to make to satisfy our new aspirations?

Peter Drucker gives us three ideals to follow:

1. Build on islands of strength and health.

2. Work only with those who are receptive to what you are trying to do.

3. Work only on those things that will make a great deal of difference if you succeed.

So, here we are at a crossroad. Will our lives be a series of temporary material successes or one of lasting significance? Are those daily activities which have seemed so important keeping us from being ourselves and giving back to society? When we choose not to be threatened by the changes before us and systematically make decisions toward our new goals, our lives can be much richer than in the past. Why?

1. We will be less likely to be diverted by things that do not matter.

2. We will finally be able to live out our own agenda rather than someone else's.

3. We will regain control of our lives.

4. We have more resources than we did as a younger man.

5. We know how to play through pain.

6. We have an opportunity for a new beginning.

Perhaps a few of my personal experiences will help clarify the importance of a life change: At about age fifty-five, I began to see that my life needed to take on new meaning. Having a wonderful wife and family, being a successful businessman, living in a nice home, and going to one black tie event after another were no longer giving me the inner satisfaction I needed. What I had not fully admitted up to this point was that acceptance—blue ribbons, rewards and awards, distinctions attained by "always doing the right things," and always winning—had been the sources of my motivation.

I was never *really* satisfied as I went from one short-lived high to the next. I began dreading the "in-between times," and the voids in my life began to affect my whole disposition. My wife urged me to begin exploring some new activities which might help bring back my old enthusiasm. My search for meaning and significance became a preoccupation, as Gail Sheehy said it would in *Passages*. It was then, while searching for this so-called new direction, that I began to experience some new anxieties. I knew I wanted and needed to be worthwhile and significant, but for the first time in my life, I felt alone and afraid, and even went so far as to question my emotional stability. I was truly living Thoreau's "life of quiet desperation."

After months of talking with my family, close friends, and therapists, I began to understand that because no one else walked in my shoes, I was really the only one who could fix my problem.

I turned to the memory of my father. He had been a coach and teacher all of his adult life, and loved every minute of it. In fact, I never knew a happier person. Money, or the lack of it, was never an important factor in his life—

he was rewarded in other ways by being a significant influence in the lives of his students.

Impressed by my father's love of teaching, I jumped at the chance when a friend arranged an interview for me at my alma mater's school of business. For awhile I served as a guest lecturer in its department of insurance, and I quickly found that teaching students the ins and outs of the insurance business was a whole lot easier than trying to sell it! It also gave me some personal satisfaction to know I was sharing my knowledge of the business with others.

Still searching for my life of significance, my wife and I started a Sunday school class for young married couples. Two years later, I began teaching a class of singles between the ages of forty and sixty. Some had never been married, many were divorced or widowed, and a few had alternative lifestyles. Most of them were in the process of climbing their own mountains, and many of their trying experiences were similar to my own. We found many of our problems and anxieties were not uncommon and looked for ways to solve them together.

Today, teaching is what has kept me motivated and upbeat because I know I am helping others. Teaching is giving new purpose to my life and has been the power behind my transition from success to significance.

Now, what about you? It is impossible to simply wake up one morning and decide to take a new direction in life.

As a way to begin, here are some questions you may want to ask yourself:

1. What would I love to do without concern for monetary reward?

2. What have I done in the past that I really loved doing?

3. If I were twenty-five years old and just getting started, what path would I follow?

Write your answers down in a spiral notebook. Put it away and reread them a week later. You may be surprised to find a pattern or connection in your answers which may be pointing toward your first new step. Remember, there are two attributes in your favor:

• You have had real life experiences.

• You can find a unique avenue to share these with others.

By becoming a significant person, you will agree with Pat M. Morley's premise that "A man's most inward need is to be significant, to find purpose and meaning." You have had all the success you need. It is time to forget about all those trophies on your wall—and in your head. This is a great time to make changes in your life which will give you a lasting legacy. Now, get moving!

>‹

Not everything that is faced can be changed, but nothing can be changed unless it is faced.

— James Baldwin

CHAPTER THREE

BEYOND AGE FIFTY: YOU SHOULD BE IN CONTROL

Time is the coin of your life. It is the only coin you have, and only you can determine how it will be spent. Be careful lest you let other people spend it for you.

— Carl Sandburg

Beyond Age Fifty:
You Should Be
In Control

Realizing the need for a passage from success to significance often comes at an unexpected moment. If we are not ready, it can be alarming. We need to realize that by age fifty, we can, and should, be in control. If not, as Carl Sandberg indicates, someone else will be.

Let's begin by taking a look at Chris, a fifty-seven-year old businessman I play golf with at least once a week. He began his career at the bottom of the ladder thirty years ago, and by long, hard work, is now a successful investment banker. He has a lovely wife, two children in prep school, two secretaries, a new Mercedes-Benz, and a nice home in a prestigious neighborhood. By the way, he is also a six-handicap golfer!

In the past year, he worked about sixty hours a week and had gained twenty-four pounds. When an annual physical disclosed a blood pressure reading of 160/110, he was placed on medication to help lower the numbers and advised to lose thirty pounds. But, Chris continued to live the good life . . . three to four glasses of wine every night and entertained clients at fancy restaurants two or three nights a week. Despite his doctor's recommendation for an exercise program, he thought the weekly round or two of golf would suffice.

After having lunch one day in the grill of his country club, he went into the men's room. As he walked past the mirror, for the first time, he stopped and took a long, hard look at the older, tired-looking man staring back at him. For the first time he recognized the huge rock which was blocking his beaten path, and agreed there was the need for change.

And so it is with most men. We are too busy to notice the passage of time. In our minds we still feel years younger than we really are, but then, suddenly one day, something causes us to realize our bodies have continued to age. While it is important to continue to be active and vibrant mentally, we must finally acknowledge that our bodies need more care . . . a workout at the gym, maybe a good massage once in awhile, and a sensible diet. You must be in control—you have some great years left.

At age fifty, Tom Brokaw wrote an essay for the *New Yorker* while he was still an NBC anchor. He started out by saying he believed every young man's fantasy was to have a fling with an older woman—A "Mrs. Robinson" type. After it occurred to him that for an older woman to be interested in him, she would be in her sixties, he said, "And, if a sixty-year-old woman decides to have a fling with a younger guy, that leaves me out!"

Sometimes the wake-up call can be sobering. It may be a good friend who dies of a sudden heart attack; a business associate, a heavy smoker, is diagnosed with cancer; or a fellow member of your breakfast club commits suicide after years of depression. "Gee, they were my same age," you say. Another real eye-opener can come when a doctor prescribes medication for your hypertension. How in the hell did this happen? Blood pressure problems are for old people, not a fifty-year-old!

What do we do now? As the title of this chapter states, *Beyond Age Fifty: You Should Be In Control.* But, are you? Here is the good news: We have choices now we did not have twenty-five years ago. We do *not have to* go to events and parties we do not enjoy; we do not *have* to eat the things we know are bad for us; we do not *have* to have a second, or even a first, drink just to be sociable; and we do not *have* to become a couch potato just because we have a few aches and pains. We have the choice.

It is never too late to make some positive changes in our lives. How well we age in this second phase of our life is determined by the changes we set in motion now. In his book, *Game Plan,* Bob Buford gives some suggestions:

1. "Delegate at work, home, and play. You cannot do everything and should not try."

This was a very difficult transition for me. Since age twenty-three, when I began my insurance career, I thought it was not only my duty, but my obligation, to do my own work, make recommendations, and completely fulfill my client's requests. I believed no one could actually do the job was well as I could. Wrong! It took years to learn that although there were certain things I could do very well, I could delegate those parts of my business to others who could do the job equally well, or maybe even better.

This also works at home or at play. If your wife is better at managing the money, let her handle it. If she is better at room arrangement, let *her* say where *she* wants the sofa. We also cannot be super-dad three hundred and sixty-five days a year. While our children may enjoy having us attend their every social and sports event, we simply cannot be everywhere all the time without wearing out fast. By limiting the number of your children's involvements and sometimes alternating between parents as to which one goes to which child's events, can be a better plan.

2. "Do what you do best; drop the rest. Go with your strengths."

Some of the things we do are easy, clear-cut, or undemanding, and, most likely, give us a positive outlook on life. Contrary to this, some things just may not be our "cup of tea." When men find themselves in a job that is not using their full capabilities, we often feel trapped and unable to make the necessary adjustments which might make us happier. Financially, we may not have the luxury of making a job or career change. However, by better utilization of our skills and talents, there may be some changes we can make in our existing job which will give us a new perspective.

Having attended seven different schools prior to high school, I interacted with all kinds of people, and developed communication skills at an early age. As a result, all of my pre-college interest tests showed I would do best in a people-oriented profession. I chose the insurance business. For thirty years I had a successful career, but after that, my enthusiasm began to decline.

Realizing this, I decided to go into insurance management and acquired a company of forty agents, a staff of twelve, *and* a new set of problems. It took awhile, but I finally concluded I did not like managing people—telling them what to do, when to do it, and setting their financial goals was not what I did best. So I hired people to do the tasks I truly disliked and returned to my routine of personal production and helping young college graduates learn the ins and outs of the business world. I found myself doing

29

again the things I liked and did best.

So go with your strengths. Delegate what you do not like to do and do not waste time with activities which produce stress, or that you do not do well.

3. "Know when to say no. Do not take on something you do not want to do or do not have the time for."

How many times have we found ourselves doing something we had no interest in, but did it anyway just because it was the "thing to do"? I regret not learning to use the "permissible 'no'" earlier in my life.

We do not have as much time as we once did to involve ourselves in activities we do not enjoy. Of course, we have family and social obligations which must be met, but we have also earned the right to limit them. Does this mean we will only do the things which fit into our plans? Absolutely not! I am, however, suggesting that you set some priorities. If you are playing golf or tennis or doing any activity just because you feel obligated, or just to let the "right people" see you, then drop it. You will find quality time for family, charities, or hobbies, and be a happier you.

One suggestion: When saying 'no', try to suggest an alternative. Suppose you and your spouse have the grandchildren for a long weekend. She wants you to go shopping with them, but shopping is not what you had in mind for the beautiful, sunny day. Instead, by offering to take the kiddos to the park, your spouse will have the afternoon off to do what she really wants to do, and, hopefully, everyone is happy. It is certainly worth a try.

4. **"Set limits. Cut back on the number of appointments you keep, leave the office on time, cut the number of business trips by half."**

We men know there are twenty-four hours in each day, but if we are not careful, someone will have us scheduled for at least twenty-three of them. By using our time more efficiently, we will be free for more activities which bring us pleasure. It is amazing how co-workers will take up our time on trivia and non-productive issues. Does this mean you cannot still be a friendly and pleasant person? Of course not. But, you are the one who can decide what is important business dialogue and not just social chit-chat. Remember, **you** are in control.

Let me suggest an experiment for you to carry out in the coming week.

Keep a log of the time you spend on true business activities and the time spent on other things. The numbers may come as a shock. I know a very successful business manager with the philosophy that he could solve most of his associate's questions in ten minutes. After ten minutes, he charged them $100 per hour. By paying him out of my own pocket a couple of times, I was impressed with the need to get my business done efficiently. So, work smarter and value your time because the clock is ticking.

5. "Protect your personal time by putting it on your calendar."

Be sure it includes regular quiet time, where you have absolute silence, for prayer and reflection.

When have you had some time in the day that was just yours, your quiet time? Unless you are already making quiet time a priority, the chances of this happening are remote. Why? Because there are so many other things going on in our lives, we forget to give ourselves this gift.

From experience, it will never happen unless *you* make it happen. It cannot be a "maybe," but rather it must be an exact time, written in on the calendar, just as if it was an appointment with your most important client or a lunch date with a friend. My experience shows it should be at the same time and same place each day so you can be assured of quietness and seclusion.

What you do during this time is personal, maybe a prayer for the day, remembering someone who needs a kind word, or perhaps simply reflecting on how to be a better person. Remember, no one is going to set this time aside for you. This is y*our* job, not one you can delegate to someone else.

6. "Work with people you like, who add energy to your life, not those who take energy away."

There are some people who make us feel good, put excitement in our life, and help direct us toward positive ideas and thoughts. Contrary to this, there are people who are always negative, complaining about every little thing. They are basically unhappy, and enjoy making others that way. We need to recognize who these people are, and stay away from their negative thoughts and attitudes. If you are the boss, this might involve firing or hiring a few. Surround yourself with honest, but optimistic, friends and associates.

7. **"Set timetables. If you fail to put your dreams on a timetable, they will quickly become unfulfilled wishes."**

If you have a dream, or a goal, write it down on paper. Then write down a timetable for carrying it through. It will never be fulfilled until you commit yourself to it. As an example, say you would like to reduce your golf handicap to twelve. By what date would you like this to become a reality? If it is now January 15, and you want to have a twelve-handicap in time for a tournament in six months, then July 15 becomes your target date. You may not make it, but unless you commit your dream to paper, chances are very slim of accomplishing it. There is something about writing goals down on paper that makes us work harder. Remember, you are the one in control!

8. **"Downsize. Think about the time and energy which is drained by owning a big house, a boat, a weekend place, two or three cars, or a club membership. None of these is bad individually,**

and may well provide some fun, but they can easily become master controllers."

It is very difficult to give up the things we have had in the past. But, at some point, our toys become liabilities. Things which were important when we were in our thirties and forties may not be now. As well, toys are expensive. The extra money it takes to maintain all our possessions can become a burden instead of a pleasure. Maybe a nice trip once a year would be more satisfying than owning a second home.

However, cutting back may not be as easy as it seems. Your children may not want to give up the weekend waterfront house; your wife enjoys the clubs you have belonged to for twenty years; and the third car? What if yours is in the shop? You need to have in-depth discussions with not only your wife, but your children. Your wife will possibly be understanding, but it can be a hard sell to the children when you tell them you are putting the ranch on the market. One solution is to give them the option of buying some of the toys which you have been paying for all these years, but which they have enjoyed. There are rarely any takers.

Downsizing is not always easy, but once we make the decision, we often wonder why we did not do it several years before. We should be in control, not controlled!

9. "Play around a little. Play should be a significant activity, not so much in terms of time spent, but in importance."

Try doing some of these things in the middle of the week, not just on the weekends:

a. Take your wife to lunch and have a bottle of wine.

b. Go to a movie in the afternoon.

c. Catch an afternoon ball game.

d. Play a round of golf with a family member.

e. Take one of your children to lunch.

f. Call a friend who lives in a foreign country.

g. Visit someone in the hospital.

h. Walk in the park—alone.

i. Write a letter, or send an e-mail, to someone who means a lot to you.

j. Visit your parents (or parent) if they are still living.

Add more of your own ideas to the list. It will make you feel good about yourself.

10. "Take the phone off the hook once in awhile."

What is the single-most distracting object in our home or office? The telephone. Thank you, Mr. Bell.

Have you ever thought about letting the answering machine do its job? Ask yourself, how important are most calls? How many of those could wait until you call back? Here is an exercise you might try for a few days. Answer every call, and keep a record of who called and what they called about. Most likely you will find you are being interrupted by many insignificant calls which either did not ever have to be answered—sales calls, solicitations, wrong numbers—or which could be returned on your time schedule. On another day, let the answering machine catch the calls and respond to the important ones. It's your time. Take control!

I would be remiss if I did not mention one more thing: Have an annual physical and listen very closely to what your personal physician tells you. Your physical and mental state must be in balance if you are to continue a life of activity and excitement. You want to be around to enjoy your grandchildren!

⌁

It is never too late to be
what you might have been.

— George Eliot

CHAPTER FOUR

UNDERSTANDING THE SIGMOID CURVE

It is one of the paradoxes of success that the things and ways which got you there are seldom those things that keep you there.

— Charles Handy

UNDERSTANDING THE SIGMOID CURVE

In Charles Handy's landmark book, *The Age of Paradox,* he devotes a chapter to the *Sigmoid Curve.*

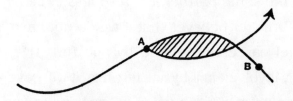

The curve illustrates the upward trend of our development, growth, and maturity, and then describes how somewhere along the way we hit a slump and begin going downhill. Handy says, "The secret to constant growth is to start a new Sigmoid Curve before the first one peters out. The right place to start that second curve is at Point 'A'

where there is the time, as well as the resources and energy, to get the new curve through its initial explorations and floundering before the first curve begins to dip downward."

The upsweep curve to get to point 'A' represents the mountains we men climb in order to get to the top. But at the summit, we begin going downhill, as represented by the descending curve to point 'B', and it is often difficult to stop. So, the aim should be not to let our lives reach a downward spiral at all.

For example, couples often fall into a monotonous routine which eventually begins to eat away at their relationship. Before recognizing the need for changes, they are already at point 'B,' and by then it may be too late for the marriage to survive. Charles Handy says, "*It is a lot easier to make changes with my present spouse than to start over with someone new. It is like a second marriage, but with the same partner it is also less expensive.*"

Peter Drucker believes that if we do not have a second or parallel career in service by age forty-five, and not vigorously involved in it by age fifty-five, it will never happen. He further states, "*If the voice is speaking to you now, do not look for reasons to ignore it. There will always be reasons to stay where you are. It is faith that calls you to move on.*" In the world of sports, we see examples of Handy's premise that many of the things and ways that get the players to the top are seldom the things which keep them there. Golf pros and coaches readily recognize this.

40

Let's suppose you are fifty years old, and a six-handicap golfer. You are long off the tee and rarely three putt. Ten years later, you are sixty years old. Your driver only takes you 210 yards, not 260 yards as before. You three putt four times during the eighteen holes. To stay at a six-handicap, you must make some changes in your game. You work more on your mid-irons, your short game, and take a few lessons in getting out of sand traps. You can now get back to the magic six, but it is not the same game that got you there ten years ago.

If success comes too early, it can be a disaster when your star begins to fade and you are still a young man. Bjorn Borg is a classic example. If he had only foreseen that winning would not be forever and had a "Plan B" ready, some of his frustrations may have been eased.

Yes, life will throw us curves. No, we do not know what tomorrow will bring. Yes, change is inevitable, but we must have courage to move forward and climb these mountains before us. Life is good. Let's keep it that way!

The future is not some place we are going, but one we create. The paths are not found, but made, and the activity of making them changes both the maker and the destination.

— John Schaar

CHAPTER FIVE

STRESS IS NOT JUST A SIX–LETTER WORD

An obstacle may be either a stepping stone

or a stumbling block.

— Anonymous

STRESS IS NOT JUST A SIX–LETTER WORD

There will always be some type of stress in our lives. Stress, defined as mental or emotional tension characterized by feelings of anxiety or fear, occurs daily. And, no one is immune. The question, therefore, becomes not if we will *experience* stress, but will we be able to *manage* it?

The bad effects of unmanaged pressure and stress are illustrated by a story of nine of the world's former most successful financiers. They all knew how to make *big money*. Twenty-five years later, a research team disclosed the following:

- The president of the largest independent steel company died in bankruptcy and lived on borrowed money for five years before his death;

- The president of the greatest utility company died penniless in a foreign land while a fugitive from justice;

- The president of the largest gas company went insane;

- The greatest wheat speculator became insolvent and died abroad;

- The president of the New York Stock Exchange had only recently been released from Sing Sing prison;

- A former member of the US President's cabinet was pardoned so he could die at home;

- The great *bear* of Wall Street committed suicide;

- The head of the greatest monopoly committee suicide;

- The president of the Bank of International Settlements also committed suicide.

All of these men had learned the art of making a living, but apparently none had learned *how to live*.

As we begin moving from success to significance and begin putting ourselves in charge and managing the events in our lives, we must look long and hard at the stress in our lives. We must learn to accept events that we cannot control and be able to turn them loose. For example, we cannot control the stock market, nor can we keep our next airline flight from being late or cancelled. Rather, it is the stress caused by too much to do, too little time, and by our instinct to micromanage everyone and everything around us.

If hypertension is the most prevalent silent killer, then stress cannot be too far behind. The problem with stress is that it can start at any age, and we will most likely not know when it is building up. Has anyone ever said to you, "You really seem stressed out," when, in fact, you really never noticed any changes in your mood or attitude? No one is immune to stress, and there are several factors which can lead us to it. The ones I personally experienced are:

1. A daily routine which I did not always control.

2. A psychological desire which pushed me to be successful.

3. The inability to say no to many people and activities in which I had no interest.

A personal experience may demonstrate how stress can affect us *and* our families: In my late forties, I worked long and hard hours, and was a person who was in tune (I thought) with my body. I played tennis, jogged, and was on a healthy diet. I weighed 160 pounds, which was within two pounds of my weight when I graduated from high school in 1954.

One morning after a three-mile jog, I had two cups of black coffee. Later on the way to the office, I suddenly developed an odd sensation in the middle of my chest. My pulse rate was high, and I could tell I had an irregular heart beat. Instead of going to the office, I drove to the office of my personal physician. Within minutes, I was diagnosed with PVC's (premature ventricular contractions). A stress EKG proved his preliminary diagnosis was correct. My condition was also confirmed by wearing a heart monitor for the next twenty-four hours.

I was told my PVC's were simply stress-related: A heavy work load, three children in private schools, and too much caffeine had pushed my stress level dangerously high. Do not let this happen to you!

It is not easy to advise someone to slow down. But, believe me, all of the *deals* we are chasing are not worth the consequences they may cause to our physical and mental health. Success is important, but being healthy to enjoy our later years is far more important. Aggressively and systematically doing away with or reducing stress-causing situations is another mountain we must learn to climb.

Over a long period of time and a lot of soul searching, I found an effective way to relieve stress. For me this involved sharing my feelings, talents, and time with others. I began by regularly visiting a friend who needed a sympathetic shoulder to lean on . . . in other words, he was not climbing his mountains very well. This new endeavor made me feel good about myself, especially when the time I spent with my friend began taking the place of some things I had previously done which were not nearly as worthwhile. Everyone needs to know they are not alone and the best way to do this is by giving the gift of our time. Visiting shut-ins, or friends in the hospital or nursing homes, is a good way to start.

Several years ago I had the opportunity to spend four hours in a stress management class taught by Dan Baker, PhD. He spoke about three principles which aid in lowering our stress levels:

1. Accept that we cannot control other people.

2. Accept that we have little or no control over many situations in which we find ourselves.

3. Know that we are not perfect.

I remember what a relief it was to hear this. I felt as though my mind had been relieved of a bunch of *junk* I had been carrying around for years . . . I realized I did not have the power or the right to make my wife and children into carbon copies of myself; I was suddenly relieved that traffic jams and flu bugs were not my fault; and, I did not have to beat myself up over a forgotten phone call.

I was equally impressed with three of Dr. Baker's explanations:

Stress Definition: *Stress can be defined as your body's response to any real or imagined demand placed upon it. Sources of stress can be environmental, physical, or mental in nature. And, not all stress is bad. Like the strings on a violin, if they have too little tension, we won't like the music; too much and the strings can break.*

49

Stress Response: *There is a physiological built-in mechanism, the arousal of the sympathetic nervous system, which helps us respond to threatening events. It is characterized by coordinating increases in oxygen consumption, blood pressure, heart and breathing rate, and amount of blood pumped to heart and skeletal muscles.*

This response was built in to us many, many generations ago when our ancestors faced saber-toothed tigers and the like; when we needed to fight or flee. There aren't any more saber-toothed tigers; we invent our own contemporary versions of them . . . letters from the IRS, traffic jams, relationship issues, unruly children, and faltering business deals.

Symptoms: *What happens if you respond to a traffic jam as though it were a saber-toothed tiger? The stress response can cause certain symptoms, exacerbate current problems, or be highly correlated with other symptoms. For instance, research suggests that asthmatics have more asthma attacks when they are stressed.*

Later in the one-on-one sessions with Dr. Baker, class participants were given an hour in which to address individual problems. Here is the one with which I felt I needed the most help:

I had an employee who for two years had made my life stressful. With sixty other employees to manage, I began resenting his daily interruptions and negativity. The first question Dr. Baker asked was, "Have you ever spoken to this individual about your specific differences, and how it is affecting you mentally?" I said we had talked in general terms but that nothing had really changed. Dr. Baker made a simple, yet powerful, suggestion:

Write your associate a letter, outlining your past differences, your conversations, and how stressful it is to work with him. Now, put the letter in the top drawer of your desk. The very next time a conflict occurs, call him into your office, hand him the letter and ask him to read it in front of you. Then say, "There is no reason to continue a relationship which is causing this emotional drainage." Wish him well in the future, and end your business dealings immediately.

A couple of weeks later, I had an opportunity to carry out that suggestion. To my surprise, the employee agreed, and we parted as friends. This was some of the best business advice I ever received. Ten years later, I met the ex-employee at a golf outing. We shook hands and laughed about why it had taken us so long to end our conflict.

The point I want to make is if stressful problems are causing you to lose sleep, worry, or get angry, ask for advice . . . then follow it. Stress is a killer: silent, but deadly! The good news, though, is that you *can* make changes.

Without knowing who we are, what we are capable of, and what things we cannot control, we can easily become disgruntled and negative. A warning: Stress most often leads to depression, so please read the next chapter very carefully.

✝

Life is 10% of what happens to you, and 90% of how you respond to it.

— Anonymous

CHAPTER SIX

DEPRESSION FROM A LAYMAN'S VIEW

In the midway of our mortal life,

I found me in a gloomy wood, astray,

Gone from the path direct.

— Dante's *Inferno* (canto XV11)

DEPRESSION FROM

A LAYMAN'S VIEW

Webster's New World College Dictionary defines depression as, "**1** low spirits; gloominess; dejection; sadness, and **2** an emotional condition, either neurotic or psychotic, characterized by feelings of hopelessness or inadequacy."

The unique symptoms and the degree of depression in a person seems directly related to how well he is dealing with the stresses, the changes made and needing to be made in his life. In this chapter I will be talking only about depression and clinical depression and will not include the complexity of manic depression.

As we look at the topic of depression, you may see yourself in one of the following categories:

55

- You have never been depressed. Perhaps there have been days when you have not felt mentally energized, but you have not experienced lingering days of being in a *down mood.*

- You have never been depressed, and believe those who are can change their mind-set and get back into a good mood by themselves.

- You have had periods of depression and not really understood your feelings and what was causing them.

- You recognize you are currently depressed, but are keeping it to yourself.

- You deny you are depressed, and believe the word *depression* has bad social connotations. "Only crazy people need a 'shrink'," you say.

- You are currently depressed, you know it, and are seeking professional help. My hat is off to you if you fall into the last category, since depression is rarely resolved without help. The bad news is you cannot cure something you do not understand. The good news is that it is curable. Believe me!

➜✦

Part I of this chapter is my own story of depression, written as honestly as I know how. I have tried to make it as clear and precise as I can without using complex scientific and medical terminology. The second part of this multifaceted problem comes from the private encounter, research, and study, by Philip Burguières. He has given permission for me to share this with you.

My goal here is two-fold: 1) To help me have a better introspection on my life (perhaps a selfish reason), and 2) If just one person reads this chapter and is helped in any way, then it, along with Philip's research, is completely worthwhile.

Part 1

This is my story

I learned the hard way, as most of us do, that a person can slip into a depressive state without really knowing or understanding what is happening in his life. It was a very slow process and came without any red flags to warn me.

It was mid-1991, and I was fifty-five years old. Everything had been moving in the right direction, or so I thought. I was married, and still am, to a wonderful, supportive lady, and had three grown children whom I adored. I was active in the community, and had just finished coaching a church basketball league for seven seasons. I lived in a nice neighborhood, my business was successful, my wife and I attended church on a regular basis, we belonged to a country club, and I played tennis two or three times a week.

Then why was I tired all the time? How could I go from being an extrovert to an introvert in the blink of an eye?

Why was it difficult to discuss my emotional changes with anyone? Why, as the downward spiral continued, did I keep hiding my feelings? I can give you two reasons: I did not acknowledge my problems because (a) I thought they were *temporary*, and (b) I did not understand how an ordinary person, with a wonderful family, good health, and financial security could feel like *hell* every day. It became routine trying to escape from my feelings of despair. I kept thinking "Hey, tomorrow *is a new day and everything will be fine."*

I found myself in overload. I wanted a place to hide where I was free from being found. As I experienced this confused state, it was very easy to blame others. I did not want any more challenges. I stared into space and walked from room to room for no reason. Bottom line: I just wanted to be left alone. Period!

Putting on a suit and tie and going to the office was a struggle. But, then something strange occurred. In about ten days, I was completely back to normal. No more anxiety about life, no bad days. But this was short-lived.

A month later I was again *mentally down . . .* except this time the feelings were deeper, more pronounced. I dreaded social activities, and my concentration level was zero. I had always been an avid reader, especially anything having to do with sports, but I even stopped reading the morning paper. I would sit in my back yard with a cup of coffee and just wonder what the day was going to bring.

Little did I know, but I was about to face the biggest mountain of my life!

I was no longer the husband and father my family knew. At my wife and children's urging, we got together one evening, and they all insisted I seek professional help. What could I do but agree? The next morning I woke at about six o'clock, and my mental state had gone from bad to worse.

My wife suggested I call a friend who had experienced a period of depression a year earlier. At half after six the next morning, I was on the phone, telling my friend I needed his help. He suggested we get together for lunch. I said, "No, I mean right now." After meeting for two hours over breakfast and multiple cups of coffee, I made an appointment for the next day with his psychologist, Debbie Longano, PhD.

The talk therapy with her was amazing. I felt better after only one hour in her office, but, I was not out of the woods yet. I had gone too far, carrying too much on my own shoulders to be cured in just one hour.

I was diagnosed as being in a mild (not *mild* to me) depressive state, and an anti-depressant was prescribed. I came out of my depressed state after about three months, but the side effects of the medication had been difficult to handle. I experienced nausea, hot flashes at night, and a near-total loss of my libido. This, in itself, was enough to make me depressed!

My help in the long run came from hourly sessions

with the psychologist who understood me and dug deep into my heart and brain. Also, physical exercise gave me not only tension relief, but also a good feeling about myself. I was on the road to recovery. It was a slow journey, but when you are depressed, each day of being better is a major step. Climbing up, rather than going downhill, gave me a whole new perspective on life.

Looking back on my bout with depression, several events added to my stress level and might have triggered my depression:

- My father had died from complications of open heart surgery.

- My mother had fallen and broken her hip, which required around-the-clock care.

- After being in charge of an international tennis event for twelve years, I was experiencing a void in my life when I asked someone else to take over.

- My insurance business was no longer challenging.

- An uncle, whom I loved and admired, was hit and killed by a drunk driver.

- My family's long history of heart disease made me apprehensive about my own heart's condition.

- My younger son had a skiing accident, which required ACL surgery.

- My older son was in a major automobile accident.

• A very close friend of forty years died after a long battle with cancer.

I believe that too many losses and concerns on top of unmanaged stress had opened the door to my condition. Many other factors can also lead to depression which, thankfully, played *no* part in my personal situation: I was, and remain, happily married, my children were on their own and doing well, and I did not turn to drugs or alcohol to alleviate my problems.

My closing words on this subject are: *You are not alone*! If your life is not going in the right direction, or if you have mood swings and are despondent, discuss these feelings with your family. Then see a professional who deals with these types of problems. Life is too short to waste even a minute!

It is also very important for you to understand how depression affects family members. Below are some comments from my children:

> *Growing up with depression when it is affecting your hero, your father, makes the puzzle even more complex and disruptive to the family unit. When your leader is wounded emotionally, all your peers, colleagues, friends, and family are affected by the trickling effects. For many years, Dad's insurance business thrived, but as it did, long hours at the office were more and more common. It was very uncomfortable*

61

to watch my father experience the mental anguish of payrolls, high rent, and quotas on a daily basis. Thankfully, with medications and time with his therapist, there was light at the end of the tunnel. Occasionally, circumstances concerning my father's depression still exist, but they are much more under control. In fact, (writing) this book has kept a smile on his face for the past few months. I love you, Dad.

—Wade Knight

>‹

I saw a very easy, outgoing person turn into someone who was easily irritated and consumed with his own thoughts. The hardest part for me was to observe the frustration he showed while trying to identify and deal with his depression. Intellectually he began to understand it, but emotionally he could not conquer it alone. As with all mental illnesses, people have a choice: ignore it or confront it. I am proud Dad chose the latter. Was this the more difficult choice? Yes. I would rather have a dad with some inconsistencies in behavior, than a dad who is completely tuned-out and detached.

—Amy Knight Miller

>‹

Prior to depression taking hold, Dad was a vibrant, energetic father whose charisma was contagious and his vigor was tireless. Depression, being the nasty misunderstood beast that it is, took hold of Dad and was apparent in the spring of 1991. It was an all-consuming disease which left him emotionally shaken, and, to a degree, physically debilitated. Dad's spirit had been broken, and his struggle to regain control began when he realized professional help was needed.

—Brady Knight

➤◆

Part 2 of this chapter explains the multifaceted problem of depression and comes from private encounters, research, and study by Philip Burguières. He has given permission for me to share the following information from his *Clinical Depression and the CEO* presentation. I would like to emphasize that the information here is only a small portion of his worldwide research on understanding the causes of depression. I am attempting to stress some pivotal points which I experienced.

Part 2

Written by Philip Burguières

So you will not feel alone, the World Health Organization estimates 350 million people are affected by depression. The number one self-treatment for depression is alcohol. My study has shown the most common signs of depression to be:

Emptiness—*Life is no longer a joy. You feel empty.*

Sadness—*Happy occasions can make you sad, and sad occasions put you in a downward spiral.*

Negativity—*The past, present, and future look bleak.*

Anxiety—*Being high-strung is a very common sign of depression.*

Apathy—*Depression and apathy are cousins. Spouses of depressed people report a loss of interest in social activities, including family life and sex.*

Guilt—*"I'm a failure. My children and spouse have problems because of me."*

Sleeplessness—*You wake up early, if you sleep at all, and are normally exhausted.*

Change in Diet—*Some people do not care about food and lose weight. However, some people do the opposite and gain weight. Making matters worse, a poor diet aggravates depression.*

Suicidal Thoughts—*When life gives you misery,*

death can seem attractive. People who are suicidal need constant supervision.

Telling a person who is depressed to "shape up" or to "pull yourself up by your bootstraps," can do real damage. You *do not* snap out of depression. Would you tell a person who has cancer to just "will it to go away?"

Causes of Depression:

Understanding mental illness is still in its infancy. To be able to understand it is close to impossible—so complex are the intermingled factors of abnormal chemistry, behavior, and genetics.

Is depression biological at its root, or is it a product of past experience and a stressful environment? Most doctors seem to agree depression is caused by a combination of chemical imbalances in the brain, environmental factors, and genetics.

I do not wish to discuss all the different types of medications which are on the market for depression, but I have used all four of these (treatments) with much success:

- The sun. Being in the sun triggers a brain hormone known as melatonin.

- Yoga. Yoga can revitalize the body and help control the mind.

- Massage. This is a great way to relax.

- Exercise. It will help improve your mood.

Hope:

Depression *can* be cured. Bill Styron made it. Mary Clare Griffin made it. Several of my close friends have made it. I made it!

Overcoming depression takes time, and everyone is different. There is no magic number of months, or even years, until a depressed person is "cured." It also takes patience, which can be particularly difficult for Type A personalities. If you do not have patience before you had depression, you will learn patience. It also takes understanding on the part of your friends and loved ones. They need to understand that you are not functioning at full capacity, even though you really want to. And, finally, it takes a great deal of hope.

There is no universal cure. You have to fashion your own cure, but there are common characteristics of learning to live with depression that I have found among over a dozen people who reached the bottom and came back to find a new job in their lives. If you or a member of your family becomes seriously clinically depressed—get help. Hospitalization, medication, and therapy may all be necessary. However, *if you can find a safe alternative to hospitalization, do it!*

After you reach some form of stabilization, try one or more of these suggestions, in no order of importance:

Take refuge in a friend or friends who have taken a similar journey. They are out there. Find your family,

community, and place. Start to grow again in v̵
ways:

- Plant a flower.
- Listen to a song.
- Watch a sunset.
- Think, imagine, and feel your way into the life of others, into their joy and sorrow. Develop empathy and compassion.

Turn outward. Help others in small ways. Spend a few minutes every day trying to relate to, or help, someone else.

- Give $5 to the guy on the corner with the sign.
- Physically touch someone you have never touched before.
- Realize that the people under the overpass are most likely mentally ill and not just bums.
- The ability to nurture, protect, and sustain someone else can create a sense of self-worth.

Believe you are "not guilty." God in his wrath has not given you this terrifying disease because you are bad. He has a plan for you, and good will come out of this suffering.

Life is about inner joy. It is not about feeling good. Perhaps we have to suffer to experience joy.

Practice solitude. This has been very difficult for me. The small voice is not going to be heard in a group setting.

Be hopeful. Hope is a virtue. Hope says that in the luminous darkness through which we travel on our human journey, we sometimes seem to be alone, but we are not alone. Hope is the most important virtue for the depressed. Sometimes it is the only thing you can cling to.

Develop a calling. To have a calling means to give something the world needs. Don't do everything. Don't try to heal the world, just do your little part.

Care for a pet. It is a small but significant release from the self-centered (narcissistic) aspect of your depression.

Know your depression triggers, and avoid them. Look separately at work, social, and intimate life. Give up the triggers.

There is a God. He loves you. Believe it.

I try to do all of the above. I fail every day.

I keep trying.

— Philip Burguières

╫

It may help someone else to know there is an end to the dark tunnel in which you wander lost and alone for so long. There is an end and an opening with a light to guide you back to the world you thought you had lost forever.

— Barbara Benziger

CHAPTER SEVEN

WHAT DO YOU WANT TO BE REMEMBERED FOR?

For no good thing ever vanishes. It is carried
forward from generation to generation.

— Pam Brown

WHAT DO YOU WANT TO BE REMEMBERED FOR?

Many of you who are reading this book are in mid-life, perhaps some younger, and some who are already past mid-life but who still have a lot more to receive *and* give. Maybe this is a good time to ask, "What is my life on this earth all about, and what kind of legacy am I going to leave?"

Remember when we were children, adults always asked, "What do you want to be when you grow up? Doctor? Lawyer? Policeman? A much more important question to ask, which you almost never hear, is "What do you want to be remembered for?" Have you asked yourself this question? Have you done some thinking about how your children, or grandchildren, will remember you?

I was first asked this at age forty, when being successful in business, making money, and winning tennis matches were big-time issues in my life . . . I had plenty of time to worry about my legacy on down the line. Wrong! Our legacy is written daily.

We cannot just sit around and wait for just the right moment to suddenly shift gears and announce, "Here I am, ready to change the world."

Paul McCartney, of Beatles fame, summed it up well in his classic song, *Yesterday*. "*Suddenly, I'm not half the man I used to be. There's a shadow hanging over me. Yesterday came suddenly.*" If we are not careful, there will be so many yesterdays in our past, we will run out of time to reflect on our lives and move to another level.

Right now we are writing our own life stories. Would we rather our grandchildren (1) take a large book from the shelf and find it full of happy moments shared with friends, family, and others who benefited from our sincere attention, or (2) read a slender volume filled with material success, anxieties, and remorse because the once all-important things were forgotten or passé, and the people we tried to impress were now not nearly as important as we once thought?

Let me challenge you with a question: How do you spend your Saturdays? You may spend them playing golf, fishing, cleaning out the garage, or watching sports events on TV. All of these activities are worthy, but you could be

72

using your Saturdays to give more meaning to your life and the lives of others with some important choices. For example, are you planning to play golf with a business client or a friend who recently lost his wife? Are you going fishing with a *good ole boy* from work or taking your son to have a day of bonding that your son will probably remember forever?

Instead of spending a whole Saturday in front of the television set watching one game or race after another, pick just one that you really want to watch and spend the remaining time volunteering as a soccer coach or referee, helping with the Boy Scouts or Big Brothers, a church fundraiser, or a local shelter.

Rather than begrudging the time spent on cleaning out the garage or a fix-it project, hire the teen on your street whose parents have recently divorced to help you. Not only will the work go faster, but your reaching out to that young man at a critical time in his life might make the difference between his coping or *going off the deep end*. In addition, sharing your Saturday plans with your wife earlier in the week and promising to leave time for eating out and a movie with her will certainly benefit your marriage, as well.

Let us assume that you are going to live to age eighty. In those years, there will have been 4160 Saturdays. But if you are now fifty-five, you have only 1300 more Saturdays to be productive and significant. Go to the store and buy a large glass fishbowl. Next, buy 1300 marbles and put them in the bowl. Each Saturday, remove one marble and throw it away. I can promise you one thing: By watching those marbles decrease, you will put more emphasis on the *really* important things in your life!

Andrew Carnegie, the great philanthropist, was once asked where his excess capital should go. He answered:

- I could over-endow my children, but this would remove their incentive to achieve.

- I could pass it on to lawyers or paid executors, but they will do with it as *they* see fit.

- Or, I could invest in causes in my lifetime which will help humanity.

As we know, he chose the last one. We do not have to be another Andrew Carnegie in order to do things which have meaning and will last.

I would like to illustrate how our actions affect the legacy we are writing on a daily basis by relating two stories: The first is about golfer Phil Mikelson. Those of you who are golfers may know that until three years ago, he was the greatest golfer alive who had never won a major tournament. After finishing in second place in the Masters several years ago, he was asked by a reporter, "Aren't you tired of being such a great golfer who can't seem to ever win the *big ones?*" Phil's reply was very clear. "What I want to be remembered for is being a good husband to my wife and a great father to my girls. Certainly I would like to win a major, but I can never live up to other's expectations. If I did that, I would always feel like a failure."

What a terrific lesson for all of us. Putting our family first can never be the wrong direction to take. After all, his family will be around long after he hits his last shot off the tee.

The second story is a very personal one. For seven years, I had been coaching church league basketball, T-ball, and soccer for boys and girls seven to twelve years old. One particular day, my seven and eight year old boys were playing a game which was scheduled to begin at 5:30 in the afternoon. Most of the mothers and dads of the team members were already in the stands when the game started. With only two minutes left to play and the score 11 to 11, one of the players, small for his age, was fouled and received a free throw. In my mind, the chances of this youngster even hitting the backboard were slim, and his making the shot was next to impossible.

As he got ready to take the foul shot, he looked toward me, and put the ball on the floor. I immediately called a timeout. (I do not know what Bobby Knight may have done under these conditions). Approaching the youngster, I asked if he had a problem. He said, "My daddy promised to be at this game, and I want him to see me shoot." Knowing his dad was not there, I told him he was most likely stuck in traffic and probably upset to be missing the game. Satisfied, the boy took the shot, made it, and yes, we won! His father called me the next day and explained he had been in an important meeting and could not get away.

About three years later, I happened to run into this man at another function, and he asked if we could visit for a minute. He told me until that night three years before, he had not realized just how important parents are to their children. His parting words were, "Coach, I have tried hard not to miss another game my son has played in." Then he added, "I want my tombstone to have written on it, 'Dad was a caring father'."

In ways large and small, loving interaction with family, friends, and even strangers will build a legacy to be proud of.

‡

One judges a man's success by the love
of his children.

—Donald J. Malouf

CHAPTER EIGHT

THE TIME IS NOW!

The function of man is to live, not to exist.

I shall not waste my days in trying

to prolong them. I shall use my time.

— Jack London

THE TIME IS NOW!

Moving into the more significant phase of your life seems like a good idea. Ahead are new opportunities, fulfilling ventures, and more time to do the things you have dreamed of for several years. You see yourself playing golf or tennis just for fun, traveling with your spouse or family just to enjoy them and create lasting memories, or being involved in civic activity or charity for the betterment of others.

But, a word of caution. This is not, nor will it be, an easy transition. In your past climb up one mountain after another, you have been accustomed to attending high level meetings, being recognized for your ideas and accomplishments, and receiving promotions, increased compensation, and perks. Your identity to a large degree has been based on your profession. It is quite an adjustment for most men to get their sense of worth from smiles, hugs, and thank you's.

My own experience has proven too much leisure time will also not give you the satisfaction you desire. When men begin cutting back on social and business activities, a large part of that time must be filled with other meaningful activities or they are headed for trouble. As popular author, Alex Comfort, writes, "Leisure is a con." We do not need voids in our lives. We must have meaning, we should give back to society, and we ought to make a difference. I am not saying you should work as long and hard as you have in the past. I am, however, urging you to listen to those small inner voices which give us inspiration and direction. It is now time for us to be significant, to do what we know is right, and most of all, to give to others.

We have all been blessed with talents we have not even used yet. Now is the time for us to stand up, take a position, and help someone else climb their mountains. The first half of your life is about conquest; the second half now needs to be about heroism. Believe me, the best is yet to come.

The time is now!

Though no one can go back and make a brand
new start, anyone can start from now
and make a brand new ending.

— Carl Bard

CHAPTER NINE

CASE STUDIES

I have missed more than nine thousand shots in my career. I have lost almost three hundred games. On twenty-six occasions I have been entrusted to take the game winning shot . . . and I missed. I have failed over and over and over again in my life.

And, that's precisely why I succeed.

— Michael Jordan,
one of the NBA's greatest players

CASE STUDIES

The following pages contain self-written testimonies from eight contributors who agreed to share some of the highs and lows of their lives.

They are included with the hope they will further enlighten, encourage, and enhance your aspirations.

╬

Contributor 1

My name is Douglas D. and am sixty-six years old. I was born in Louisiana, and in the last class to attend an all male public high school. In college, while carrying a class load of twenty hours with an engineering major plus ROTC classes, I waited tables four hours a day for three meals and 50¢ an hour. After college and a brief stint in the Army, I became a sales engineer for a major corporation, and later turned to commercial real estate.

I retired in 1999 because I felt worn out and dull. I was aware the younger brokers were getting the exciting, more lucrative opportunities, while I was still working on menial deals. And worse, I knew I was not working as hard as I once did.

Upon full retirement, I had the strong need to do something so I would not become dissatisfied, unhappy, and depressed. Because of its strong volunteer program, I turned more and more to my church where I had already served as an usher for many years. I also became a classroom assistant at a local elementary school, but despite this, I have a feeling I am not doing enough to help others.

I have recently become a starter/marshall at a golf course for which I receive all of my golfing privileges, meals, and discounts on golf equipment and clothes. I currently play golf three times a week and tennis once or twice a week, and serve on the board of a tennis club. But still there are times, especially during days of bad weather, when I feel somewhat lost and depressed.

In summary, I have a strong commitment to my current set of goals: *a stronger belief and loyalty to my religion, *more activities which involve helping others, *better physical conditioning, and, most important *a stronger, warmer relationship with my wife, my three children, their spouses, and five grandchildren.

→←

Contributor 2

My name is Edmond S., and I am sixty-four years old. Even as a very young child, I wanted to be a doctor, and entered medical school prior to my senior year in college.

My wife and I married during my first year in med school. After a two-year hitch in the Army, we settled in Virginia where we have lived ever since. I began my practice with high hopes and great expectations in association with two older physicians.

However, after a year, I became unhappy and opened my own solo practice. This would not have been possible without the support and encouragement of my wife. Looking back on the following twelve years, and from a professional point of view, they were the best years of my life. Ultimately, it was necessary to bring in a younger partner, and eventually ended up merging with several other doctors. My other choice would have been to go back into a single practice, which was not a good idea at my age (sixty at the time) or retire, which I was not then mentally prepared to do.

As time moved forward, I had to come to grips with the idea of retirement. I no longer wanted to take night calls, and after lengthy negotiations with my partners, we agreed that after two years of not pulling night call duty, I would be expected to retire. Surprisingly, I didn't object to the provision.

As the day approached, I began to ask myself, "What am I going to do?" A retired attorney gave me some good advice: Do not accept any volunteer positions for at least a year. I am now a year and a half into retirement, and am loving it. I am never bored. What do I do with my time? Yard work, chores around the house, reading, and I play a fair amount of golf, although not nearly as much as I thought I would. I belong to a book club and also play bridge with a group of men every Monday.

My wife and I enjoy traveling and have taken some nice trips since I retired. One of the biggest and most intangible factors in my enjoyment of retirement is that my wife and I have fun together and enjoy each other's company. At the same time, we give each other space, and continue to pursue activities apart from one another.

As I look back on my career, I feel a sense of pride. I did what I had always wanted to do, and really enjoyed it. The bottom line is that retirement was the right thing for me to do at the time I did it, and I have no regrets. As I have said many times, "I wanted to walk out the door; I didn't want to get pushed."

➤⬩⬥⬩⬅

Contributor 3

My name is Kurt D., am fifty-three years old, and am an alcoholic and a drug addict. I grew up in a large Texas city, attended its oldest and most prestigious prep school, and graduated from a New England university with a degree in engineering. Having been born into a socially prominent family, in addition to an education, I acquired all the social skills required of a young gentleman.

I was taught that the hallmarks of a successful life were money and acceptance into society, and I pursued them with zeal. Through hard work, inheritance, and shrewd investing, I reached the top by age forty-four.

I thought I had it all . . . a beautiful wife and kids, the big house and bank account, and all the right friends and acquaintances. In reality, I had nothing except a full-blown case of both alcoholism and drug addiction.

I began drinking and drugging at age fifteen, and never looked back. I drank to get drunk, and smoked dope to get high. In these ways, I could alter my mood and escape reality. I was wittier and smarter. I easily fit into any social situation. This worked for twenty-nine years.

And then, it stopped working. I had become a zombie—burned out from abusing prescription opiates and tranquilizers. Alcoholism/addiction is a progressive disease, an obsession of the mind and a compulsion of the body. I could not stop and had lost the power of choice.

God finally intervened. My wife confronted me and checked me into a treatment facility where I stayed for four months. The hell of detox is impossible to describe. It was the hardest thing I have ever done. When the drugs finally left my system, twenty-nine years of suppressed emotions came out all at once. I was so emotionally flooded I thought I would lose my sanity. But, I didn't. I think God had something else in mind.

Things did not work out as I had hoped. In my tenth month of recovery, my wife asked for a divorce. I found my self alone, but, well, not quite. I still had the support of Alcoholics Anonymous and the love of God.

Through the programs of both AA and Al-Anon, I am learning how to be a mature adult with healthy relationships, for in the end, they are the only things of value in my life.

To that end, my purpose these days is to try and carry the message of recovery to the addict/alcoholic who still suffers. In this way I can give the gift of sobriety to those who want it in the same way it was so freely given to me. It is a tall order. In the seven years of my recovery, I have seen many die from this cunning and powerful disease. So few make it. Why have I? No idea, but I keep going because in order to keep the gift of sobriety, I have to give it away.

➤◄

Contributor 4

My name is Gilbert W., and I am seventy-one. I grew up on a farm in Mississippi, which means I started to work at an early age. I entered college at age sixteen, and after graduating in 1956, secured a job with a company in Georgia. This was the beginning of a forty-two year career with the same company, with the exception of a tour of duty with the US Army.

After being transferred to an office in Texas, I met my future wife. We married in 1963. Soon afterward, I developed a serious problem with my left eye, and eventually lost the sight in that eye. However, it was a medical problem which did not have an adverse effect on my relationship with the company. I worked long, hard hours, and this did not go unnoticed.

I was later transferred to another office as a supervisor and later as an assistant manager. In my company, the ultimate goal was to become a branch manager and share in the profits. In 1965, I was promoted to the position of branch manager in another city, where I remained for eight years. Those eight years were good for me and my family. We were active in our church and the community, built a new home, our two children were born, and business was good.

Then in 1972, I was asked if I would like to manage another office, which meant a huge step up from the one

I currently managed. We moved, and within a year, the new office became one of the largest in the company. I worked hard,but fortunately, loved it and enjoyed going to work each morning. I remained in the position of general manager for twenty-five years, and saw many changes in our particular business and the company.

In 1998, I developed some heart problems, and there were changes being made in the company which I did not like. Deciding this would be a good time to retire, I did so and have never regretted my decision.

I had not made any after-retirement plans. But being raised on a farm, I enjoyed growing plants, so six months after retiring, I decided to enroll in a twelve-week master gardener program sponsored by the county. I planned to use the knowledge I gained just in my own garden, but I enjoyed the course so much I became active in the organization by serving as a class coordinator. Later I served on its board and later as president.

I also work with second and third grade students by preparing gardens and teaching them how to grow vegetables. Last year, several of us prepared a community garden and gave over three thousand pounds of vegetables to a local food bank.

In addition to these activities, I serve as an elder and on various committees in my church and am involved with a Samaritan counseling center. I read, fish, and play a little golf. The point is I must stay busy. After working almost all my life, I cannot just sit and do nothing. There is no doubt I feel best when I am occupied with something I consider worthwhile. I feel even better when my activities help other people. That's what it's all about.

✦

Contributor 5

My name is Adam G., and I am seventy-five years old. After graduating from a university in Oklahoma with a degree in engineering, I spent two tremendously maturing years serving as a second lieutenant with the Army Corp of Engineers.

While spending the Christmas holidays with my parents a month before exiting the service, my Dad, owner of a small general contracting business, asked for my help in preparing a bid for a school building. We were the success-ful bidders, and Dad took the position 'you bid it, you build it.' This statement changed the course of my life. Going from a training engineer for a large company in a large city to a small builder in a small town was a decision I have never regretted.

During the beginning years of my business life, I was encumbered with the lack of discipline and future goals. I attempted to rectify this by entering into a marriage which was doomed to fail from the beginning, and did after a few years. During this time, business was progressing well until the mid-1960s when a major industry moved out of town. Consequently my business began to suffer.

By the late 1960s, things began to improve. I remarried, and we started a family. Business was expanding, and over the next thirty years, I launched three other corporations which complemented my contracting business. Through the 90s, these companies maintained a steady growth.

After my sons graduated from college, I encouraged them to experience the business world on their own before returning to the family business. By 1999, I realized both boys had progressed into competent leaders and wanted to expand our businesses. I decided to retire.

Retirement did not really slow me down, it only permitted me to do the things I always wanted to do—a lot of golf, racquetball, a couple of weeks a year on the ski slopes, and quail hunts with my friend in Texas. My wife and I like to travel, so we occasionally take tours and cruises. We also plan part of our life around our family and grandchildren.

My wife and I helped establish a wonderful new church in our area. I was instrumental in constructing a new church building, and because of the growth of the church, also a new expansion, all in the last ten years.

The life of retirement has many favorable advantages and good opportunities if you look for them and use them. With two little Scotties, a maintenance-free house, socially active life, grandchildren, and good friends—who could ask for anything more?

>‹

Contributor 6

My name is Travis W., and I have just turned 70. I was born in Texas, and have lived here all my life. My first marriage in 1960 began on a high note, followed by the birth of my first daughter in 1966. This high continued through 1968 when my son was born and I graduated from college. Not long afterward, however, problems in my marriage began, but another high came along after the birth of my second daughter in 1972.

In 1974, I faced an immense amount of anxiety when I decided to start my own company. Two years later, I was significantly relieved when financial statements revealed the company was well on the road to becoming successful. While I experienced highs in my business in the years of 1977 to 1989, my marriage problems continued and finally ended after a very bitter divorce.

In 1990, I met and married a wonderful woman . . . a definite high then, and it still is today. But shortly afterward, the death of my parents a year apart, the failure to secure an IPO for my company, new business struggles following 09/11, and being diagnosed with lymphoma put me at the lowest level I had ever experienced.

In 2004, my company began its recovery, as did I. After an intense regimen of chemotherapy, my doctors pronounced me in total remission in early 2005. My wife and I celebrated this good news by taking a six-week trip to Europe. Ecstatic is the only word which comes to mind in order to describe my mental and emotional attitude at this time.

In early 2006, I successfully opened two new companies in other states, both of which are well on their way to generating a profitable year.

I enjoy working more every day, and at least for now, have no plans to retire. I only wish I was thirty years old again, but with the knowledge I have gained over my years in business. It would be interesting to see the outcome.

><

Contributor 7

I am Jonas D., age 80. During the late 1970s and early 1980s, with oil at $40 a barrel, the economies of Texas, Oklahoma, and Louisiana expanded at a rapid rate. I personally expanded my firm to nineteen people.

During this time, my six children grew up and were on their own and on two occasions, I underwent serious surgery. Then oil prices began to drop, leveling at $26 a barrel, and in 1985 plunged to $10 a barrel. Energy companies were in real trouble, as well as real estate and banks. All of this caused great economic distress, physical stress, and mental depression, not only for myself, but for the others who were all in the same boat.

When I was fifty-three, I worked four days a week, and spent Friday, Saturday, and Sunday at my farm. By the time I would reach fifty-five, I planned to work three days a week, and spend Thursday through Sunday at the farm. By sixty, my plan called for me to be virtually retired.

But what actually happened?

- In November 1979, I had open heart surgery and came close to death.

- I returned to work three months later and spent Friday through Sunday at my farm.

- I lost a key man in my firm, replaced him with two, and lost them as well.

- My business began to take a plunge in 1983 and continued to get worse each month.
- I worked harder than ever before and worked five days a week.
- I had open heart surgery again in September 1984.
- After this surgery, I suffered great depression, and at the same time, the economy drifted into hard times.
- My firm was without income for three years.

Had my mental condition continued to slide as the oil prices did, I probably would not be here today. Throughout that time, I tried to keep my ship afloat with constant activity and by manipulating my mental attitude daily. I knew if I could keep busy and keep a positive attitude, I could and would survive.

Anyone can do well in good times . . . the ones who can survive the bad times can do extraordinary things in the good times. However, keeping an optimistic attitude is easier said than done. If your attitude is not good, it is very difficult to work. Getting out of bed every morning, pumping up your attitude, and calling on people for business is an *absolutely* difficult job.

Many years ago, I read this quote in a *Reader's Digest* magazine: "Don't wait for inspired moments. Work every day or you may miss them." It has helped me work each day, despite how I felt. I worked hard during those extraordinarily difficult years. Each day I said to myself, "Keep your attitude on a positive vein all day long, just this day," and each morning I asked God to help me keep a good attitude for just that day.

Because of my persistence, I got my head screwed back on properly, and since then my business has increased at an excellent rate. My debt is paid off, my taxes are current, zero corporate debt, and my employees are receiving large bonuses.

So, as I approach my sunset years, what do I need and want? I do not want to retire to my farm; I do not want to spend my days playing golf; and I do not want to travel all the time. What I do want is to stay healthy, so I work out daily. I do want to feel productive, so I work at my office three days a week. I do want to be with my beautiful wife, my children and grandchildren, and I am on a daily basis. I do want to help Houston and Texas, so I work hard at being on fire, enthusiastic, and productive . . . and at eighty I am happy today. In order to become a mature person, longevity alone is not the answer, although it helps.

Therefore, keep your body and mind alert, and remember, "When you want to sharpen a knife, you have to rub something sharp against it."

➤❖❮

Contributor 8

My name is Russell M., and am about to turn seventy. I graduated from high school in 1954 and a major university in 1958. Following graduation from law school in 1961, I accepted a position with a large prestigious firm where I made it known I was interested in becoming a trial lawyer.

I began in the trial department where I worked exclusively with the co-head of that group for six months and during that time, my interest in trial work intensified. In less than a year, I was assigned to work as a "mole" for a lawyer whose docket consisted of around two hundred cases. My job was to assist him with whatever he saw fit . . . whether it was hearing a motion, taking depositions, writing briefs, or trying cases.

I began to write his briefs on my own and was given the privilege of assisting him in trials by putting on and cross-examining witnesses. I tried my first case on my own in late 1963. In the following years, the cases I was assigned became more and more difficult, and I found myself representing several large corporations. Between 1963 and 1968, I must have tried to jury verdicts about sixty-five or seventy cases. And, in so doing, had the time of my life!

My life changed for the better in 1966 when my first child was born, and again in 1969 when the second one came. I was blessed with a caring and understanding wife who had no problem with my strenuous work requirements while she raised our children.

In 1968 I was assigned my own "mole," a bright law graduate whose passion to learn the correct trial process equaled mine. I became a partner in the firm in January 1971, and in January 1983, at age forty-six, I was made a senior partner.

In the summer of 1983, I became head of the trial department. I had been traveling for the past ten years, and an important factor in accepting this new job was that it would keep me at home. I wanted to spend more time with my wife and children.

I also served on the executive committee and in 1985 became involved in opening an office for our firm in another large city which took an enormous amount of my time. Although the number of cases I was actually trying was few, many were complex and interesting. But, I was getting tired. After thirty years of work, and at age fifty-five, I had achieved my dream of becoming a first-class trial lawyer.

In 1989 my first wife died. I remarried in 1991, and during the next three years, worked on several cases which had landed in our offices in two other cities. This involved more travel than I wanted I had just turned fifty-nine, and was now more than tired. Reflecting upon my career at this time, I realized trying lawsuits had not been fun for me in many years.

My firm had an early retirement option which could be exercised at age sixty, and it was then I started thinking seriously about taking it. But what would I do then? I decided to write a novel, and around the same time, I heard a sermon on a subject with which I strongly disagreed. I started to work in earnest on my book, and immersed myself in the study of religious history. In 1996, I was diagnosed with prostate cancer, followed by complications which lasted for six months.

Since the early 1990s, my law firm had sponsored an elementary school whose students were underprivileged minorities. In the year before retiring, I started tutoring a Hispanic third grader, and found the experience to be extremely rewarding.

That same year, I played in a charity golf tournament to raise money for a non-denominational Christian organization dedicated to assist children who were being raised in a crime and drug infested part of the city. I learned a great deal about its programs and mission, began to tutor a young African-American boy, and ultimately became heavily involved in the organization by serving on its board and providing financial support . . . and began to discover there could be life after retirement.

Since 1999 I have been in a courtroom on only two occasions, both times to witness the swearing in of two judges who had been my associates and partners.

What would my life be like now if I had not retired from the practice of law at age sixty-one instead of hanging in until retirement became mandatory at sixty-five? Without a doubt, I would not have had time to devote to tutoring which has brought me many new challenges. Would I have completed and published my novel? Probably. Would I have undertaken the intensive study of religion? Maybe.

Was my decision to retire early the right one for me? Clearly so! While some people describe their retirement years as boring or depressing, the opposite is true for me. Mine have only been invigorating and life-restoring.

><

You can't turn back the clock . . . but you can wind it up again.

—Anonymous

Winston Churchill, in an address at Westminster
College, said, "Kites rise highest against the
wind." Numerous leaders have remarked
that only a handful of individuals really mold
and affect your life.
I truly believe this is an accurate analysis.

Tributes

The following people put wind in my sails, gave me hope, made me dream, and motivated me:

My father—Dad was not only a strong influence on my life, but he was an inspiring teacher, coach, and father for fifty years. Making money was never a subject in the times we spent together. The creeds he taught me were to be a man, a good husband, a caring father, and never spend more than you make.

>←

My mother—Muggsy was the dearest and most loving person I have ever known. I know she is in heaven now, feeding her homemade food to everyone around the table. She was special, and gave me love every day of her life.

>←

Matt Hall Benton—Everyone has a person who is special to them, who is your friend when you are up, but a better friend when you are down; someone to whom you can share your interests and feelings; someone who is only a phone call away. I loved Matt for what he stood for: principles and family values. Someday another Matt may come along, but I predict it will take a very long time.

Dunbar Chambers—He would be your first call if you needed an immediate solution for any personal problem. He has experienced his share of difficulties, but always finds the time to help others.

Doug Dalton—Every man needs a friend who you know you can count on three hundred sixty-five days a year. I have never heard him say a negative word about anyone, but I have seen him lose his cool in mixed doubles a few times. He is one of a kind.

Jack Dulworth—My wife refers to him as a true Renaissance man. He recognizes beauty in all things and exhibits kindness to everyone.

Leo Kissner—When a man faces adversity, he can react in different ways. Knowing Leo and being around him during some tough times gave me a better perspective on life.

✦

Johnny Madden—If you need a good companion for bird hunting, a game of golf, or just a person who cares, Johnny fits all of these categories. Men respect other men who love their family and Big John leaves no doubt about where his family fits into his life.

✦

Ron Morris—A minister, a friend, and a true believer in the principles by which all men should live. Ron taught me what prayer means, how to pray, and what prayer in your life can do.

✦

Harry Parten—A graduate engineer who was a head tennis pro for thirty years. I learned from Harry not to cave in to the demands of an individual, but instead, do what is best in the long run for the majority. Years of working with Harry made me realize he was right—you do not have to be popular to excel.

Carl Tagge—The best businessman and finest motivator I have ever known. He took me at age twenty-three and taught me ways to go as far as I wanted in the world of business without ever compromising myself or my principles. Carl was my mentor for thirty years.

James Turnbow—I have known Jim for fifty-five years. During this time, we were high school classmates, business associates, and golf partners. His total honesty and integrity has always been a model for me to emulate. He encouraged me to lift my sights.

Don Turner—If ever a man has climbed mountains, it is Don. He is the most loyal buddy a man could ever wish for, and gives hope to all those who have lost loved ones.

I have seen where these men have been and witnessed how they all survived. They are special to me because without their love, counsel, and inspiration, my kite would never have had the wind to fly higher. Trying to lift myself to their standards put excitement in my life and gave me the desire to help others. We all need to keep moving, grow stronger, and continually learn from others. Every mountain can be climbed, but only if we use the very best resources—our friends and family.

SUGGESTED READING

Age Of Paradox, The—Charles Handy

Bible, The

Clinical Depression And The Ceo—Philip J. Burguières

8 Weeks To Optimum Health—Andrew Weil, M.D.

Enduring Classics Of Billy Graham, The—Billy Graham

Flow: The Psychology Of Optimal Experience—Mihaly Csikszentmihalyi

Game Plan—Bob Buford

Greatest Generation, The—Tom Brokaw

Half Time—Bob Buford

How To Balance Competing Time Demands—Doug Sherman and William Hendricks

I Don't Want To Talk About It: Overcoming the Secret Legacy of Male Depression—Terrence Real

Just As I Am—Billy Graham

Life Is Not A Game Of Perfect: Finding Your Real Talent and Making It Work For You—Dr. Bob Rotella and Bob Cullen

Living In The Lions Den: How to Cope With Life's Stresses—Paul L. Morell

Man In The Mirror, The—Patrick M. Morley

Meditations For Men Who Do Too Much—Jonathon Lazear

Men In Mid-Life Crisis—Jim Conway

Norman Vincent Peale: Words That Inspired Him—Norman Vincent Peale

Rest Of Your Life, The—Patrick M. Morley

Seizing The Moments: Making The Most Of Life's Opportunities—James W. Moore

Seven Seasons Of A Man's Life, The—Patrick M. Morley

Stuck In Halftime—Bob Buford

There Is Life After Stress—James W. Moore

Transitions: Making Sense Of Life's Changes—William Bridges

Understanding Men's Passages: Discovering The New Map of Men's Lives—Gail Sheehy

Utmost For His Highest, The—Oswald Chambers

BIBLIOGRAPHY

Bridges, William. *Transitions: Making Sense of Life's Changes.* (DaCapo Press, 2004). ISBN 073820904X.

Brokaw, Tom. *The Greatest Generation.* (Random House Trade Paperbacks, 2005). ISBN 0812975294.

Buford, Bob. *Game Plan.* (Zondervan, 1999). ISBN 0310229081.

Buford, Bob. *Half Time.* (Zondervan, 1999). ISBN 0310215323.

Buford, Bob. *Stuck in Halftime.* (Zondervan, 1999). ISBN 0310235839.

Burguières, Phillip J. *Clinical Depression and the CEO.* (EMC Holdings, 2001). ASIN B0006RW2FS.

Chambers, Oswald. *The Utmost for His Highest: An Updated Edition in Today's Language.* (Discovery House Publishers, 1992). ISBN 0929239571.

Conway, Jim. *Men in Mid-Life Crisis.* (Chariot Victor Publishing, 1997.) ISBN 1564766985.

Csikszentmihalyi, Mihaly. *Flow: The Psychology of Optimal Experience.* (Harper Perennial, 1991). ISBN 0060920432.

Graham, Billy. *Just As I Am.* (Harper San Francisco, 1999). ISBN 0060633921.

Graham, Billy. *The Enduring Classics of Billy Graham.* (W Publishing Group, 2004). ISBN 0849918219.

Handy, Charles. *The Age of Paradox* (Harvard Business School Press, 1995). ISBN 0875846432.

Lazear, Jonathon. *Meditations for Men Who Do Too Much.* (Fireside, 1992). ISBN 0671759086.

Moore, James W. *Is There Life After Stress? (Dimensions for Living, 1999).* ISBN 0687074819.

Moore, James W. *Seizing the Moments: Making the Most of Life's Opportunities.* (Abingdon Press, 2001). ISBN 0687015529.

Morell, Paul L. *Living in the Lion's Den: How to Cope With Life's Stresses.* (Abingdon Press, 1992). ISBN 0687222958.

Morley, Patrick M. *Getting to Know the Man in the Mirror.* (Man in the Mirror, Inc., 2000). ISBN 0967912202.

Morley, Patrick M. *The Rest of Your Life.* (Zondervan, 1998). ISBN 0310217679.

Morley, Patrick M. *The Seven Seasons of a Man's Life.* (Zondervan 1998). ISBN 0310217644.

Peale, Norman Vincent. *Norman Vincent Peale: Words That Inspired Him.* (NVP Inspirational Press (NY) 1994). ISBN 0884861007.

Real, Terrence. *I Don't Want to Talk About It: Overcoming the Secret Legacy of Male Depression.* (Scribner, 1998). ISBN 0684835398.

Rotella Dr., Bob and Bob Cullen. *Life Is Not a Game of Perfect: Finding Your Real Talent and Making It Work for You.* (Simon & Schuster, 1999). ISBN 0684842866.

Sheehy, Gail. *Understanding Men's Passages: Discovering the New Map of Men's Lives.* (Ballantine Books, 1999). ISBN 0343406907.

Sherman, Doug and William Hendricks. *How to Balance Competing Time Demands.* (Navpress, 1989). ISBN 0891092277.

Weil MD, Andrew. *8 Weeks to Optimum Health.* (Ballantine Books, 1998). ISBN 0449000265.

PERMISSIONS

I have made every effort to give credit to the ownership of all copyrighted materials quoted in this book.

✦✦

Special thanks are given to

Richard D. Fisher, Sunracer Publications, for his incredible photograph of Los Pilares in the Upper Rio Conchos, northern Sierra Madre, Mexico, which appears on the cover.

Megan Thompson for her photograph of the author.

About the Author

Granville Knight, Jr., a native Houstonian, holds a BA degree in business administration from the University of Houston. Upon graduation in 1959, as one of twenty-four men selected nationwide, he served as an officer in the Counter Intelligence Corps. Two years later, he returned to Houston and began a successful insurance career which spanned forty years.

In 2005, he was presented the *Benjamin N. "Woody" Woodson Award* which is given in recognition of meritorious service to the insurance industry and the community.

Granville has served on the boards of numerous civic organizations, as an advisory director for two major

Houston banks, and has been a guest lecturer for the University of Houston's School of Business. As well, for five years he served as chairman of the River Oaks Country Club International Tennis Tournament.

Several years ago, he began an in-depth study of problems men face in adjusting to changes in their lives. This book is based not only on his own personal experiences, but includes information he gathered from interviews and conversations with men who have faced the challenges of stress, confusion, self-doubt, and depression.

Now retired from corporate life, Granville's time is spent as a motivational speaker and Sunday School teacher. Married for forty-three years, he and his wife, Elaine, enjoy playing golf and entertaining friends on their South Texas ranch. They have three children and three grandchildren.